Slam Dunk
Magician

Phil Kettle
illustrated by Craig Smith

Black Hills

Distributed in
the United States of America
by Pacific Learning
P.O. Box 2723
Huntington Beach, CA
92647-0723

Website:
www.pacificlearning.com

Published by Black Hills
(an imprint of Toocool Rules
Pty Ltd)
PO Box 2073
Fitzroy MDC VIC 3065
Australia
61+3+9419-9406

First published in the United States by Black Hills in 2004.
American editorial by Pacific Learning in 2004.
Text copyright © Phillip Kettle, 2001.
Illustration copyright © Toocool Rules Pty Limited, 2001.

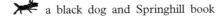 a black dog and Springhill book

Printed in China through Colorcraft Ltd, Hong Kong

ISBN 1 920924 00 0
PL-6204

10 9 8 7 6 5 4 3 2   08 07 06 05

Contents

Tony

Dog

Bert

Toocool

Chapter 1
Behind the Scenes

It's the NBA championship. The final game of the series is at Madison Square Garden. I'm one game away from winning the championship. The crowd is cheering for me.

"Toocool! Toocool! Time to get up!" Mom called.

Rats! Another really good dream interrupted.

"Toocool! Tony! Get out of bed. If you're late for school, Tony won't be allowed to spend the night again," yelled Mom.

Tony always slept like a log.
I shook him.

"Wake up," I said. "Today's
the big game."

"We should eat a big breakfast," I said. "We have our big championship game today. Team Toocool takes on Team Tony."

We ate our eggs and each drank a glass of orange juice— just what all famous basketball stars have for breakfast.

Then we raced back to the locker room to get ready.

The tension was building.
My heart beat faster.

We put on our uniforms.

"Have you ever seen a
better looking basketball player?"
I asked Tony.

The bathroom was the last stop before the game. Without looking I reached for the toothpaste. I started to brush my teeth.

Yuck! What was that? I spat all over the mirror. Oops! I'd used Dad's shaving cream instead of toothpaste.

I stayed cool anyway.

I shook hands with Tony, picked up the basketball, and opened the locker-room door. We were ready—ready to run onto the court, ready for the screams of the crowd.

Chapter 2
Facing the Crowd

It was time to become an NBA championship legend.

"Don't you dare bounce that ball inside!" said Mom.

I spun the basketball on one finger. We jogged through the kitchen and out the back to the court.

The crowd started to whistle as soon as we came into view. The chant went up.

"We want Toocool.
We want Toocool."

I waved to my fans.

Bert the Rooster and a few hens were right in the middle of the court. Dog chased them into the stands. Dog was playing for Team Tony.

10

I took my practice shots.
I was sinking them from
everywhere. Brick Wall
and I made a great team.

The crowd was
getting restless. It was time
for the game to start.
Tony looked nervous.

Chapter 3
The
Championship

The game began. I tossed the ball up for tip-off. I leaped up and tapped it to myself.

I ran around Tony. I passed the ball to Brick Wall. Then Brick Wall passed it right back to me.

Two steps and I took a long shot. The ball dropped.

Nothin' but net!

The crowd roared. Tony was stunned. Maybe he needed a new coach.

The first points were on the scoreboard. Team Toocool was in the lead.

I dribbled the ball down
the court. One bounce,
two bounces. A sharp
pass to Brick Wall.

Brick has the quickest
hands I have ever seen.
He always makes lightning
returns. Brick never, ever,
holds the ball.

I took a risk. I made a blind turn around Tony, and there was Dog!

Over I went. I'm sure Dog tripped me on purpose.

I got two free throws. They both sailed through the hoop. The buzzer sounded.

It was halftime. Would Team Tony make a comeback in the second half?

Chapter 4
The Second Half

We jogged off the court. I sat on the sidelines, eating an orange. Tony drank water. It was a hot game.

"Don't get orange juice on that shirt," called Mom.

Unbelievable! Even in the middle of an NBA game, Mom treated me like an ordinary kid.

16

The buzzer went off. It was time for the second half.

The crowd went back to their seats. The chant went up.

"We want Toocool. We want Toocool."

I threw my orange peel over my shoulder.

Toocool was back.

I raced down the court.
I threw the ball. It headed
straight for Bert the Rooster.
He was still scratching around
on the court. He had not heard
the buzzer.

Bert saw the ball coming and screeched. He dodged out of the way as fast as he could.

The rest of the crowd panicked. Dog ran up and down the court, barking his head off.

Tony made a T with his hands to call for a time-out.

The score was tied. Both teams were worried.

Chapter 5
Under Pressure

A call came from the house, "Toocool, make sure you do all your chores."

Was she kidding? There wasn't time for chores!

Now the pressure was really on. I had to score—fast.

I ran the ball down the side
of the court. It was time for
Toocool's magical
slam dunk.

Brick was standing still.
He hadn't moved an inch.
I took the chance.

With one foot in the middle of Brick's back, I flew into the air. I spun. The hoop was right in front of my eyes. I slammed the ball through it!

The final buzzer rang from the kitchen. The crowd ran onto the court. I ran around giving high fives. I was the NBA champion. I was a legend.

Chapter 6
The Legend
Lives On

Cameras were flashing. The Toocool team song was booming. I grabbed a piece of chalk and scribbled autographs for the crowd.

In all the excitement I had forgotten Tony.

I pushed my way through the crowd. I found Tony. He was signing autographs, too.

I grabbed his hand and shook it. Sports legends never forget their friends.

The crowd was leaving. I stood there enjoying my moment of success.

It was a brief moment.

"Toocool, Tony—you two need to clean up or you'll both be late for school."

Well, at least I could say I had won the final of the NBA championship. Even better, I had done it all before school.

Mom came out to wave good-bye. "Remember to clean that writing off the wall as soon as you get home from school."

What a thing to say to an NBA champion!

We got on our bikes. Tony gave the signal. Our usual race to school had begun.

I was a legend on the basketball court. I wondered how I would fare out in the great ocean on my next adventure.

The End!

Toocool's
Basketball Glossary

Chant—A chant is a simple song that repeats the same words over and over again.

Dribble—To dribble the ball is to bounce it while walking or running.

Free throw—A free throw is when you get to take a shot at the basket, without any of the opposite team trying to block you. You get a free throw if the other team fouls you while you are shooting a basket.

Slam dunk—A slam dunk is when you jump really high and slam the ball through the hoop.

29

Toocool's Backyard
Basketball Stadium

Kitchen

Locker
Room

The TV
Living
Room

Toocool's Quick Summary
Basketball

Basketball was created in America in 1891. When it first started it only had thirteen rules. Today it has hundreds of rules.

Each team has five players on the court. The game always starts with the tip-off—that's when the referee throws the ball up between two players. Each player jumps up and tries to tap the ball to a teammate. People also call this the jump ball.

Throwing the ball into the hoop is called shooting. The team that shoots the most balls through the hoop wins the game. Basketball shots earn different points. A free throw earns one point for each basket. A normal shot during the game earns two points. A shot from twenty feet away from the basket earns three points.

There are three ways to move the ball in basketball. You can pass it, dribble it, or shoot it. You can't run or walk with the ball unless you dribble it at the same time.

The **Basketball** Court

Guard

Free → Throw Line

Center

Circle

Guard

Forward

Three-Point Line

Center

The Basket
(Slam Dunk
Zone)

Forward

Sideline

Q & A with Toocool
He Answers His Own Questions

Some players have favorite positions. Which one is yours?

My favorite position is center. Usually the tallest person gets to play center. I'm not always the tallest, but I am always the best. My team needs me to play center because I'm so great at getting the jump balls at tip-off.

I also like playing guard. That way I get to use my amazing ball-handling skills. I'm an expert forward, too. I can shoot from just about anywhere on the court.

Where did you learn your magical slam dunk?

I started by watching the NBA championship players. I watched them very closely. Then Dad put a small hoop on the back of my bedroom door. I had a mini-basketball. I practiced over and over. Sometimes I practiced during the night when everyone thought I was asleep. Then, on my birthday, I got a real outdoor hoop and a full-size ball. The rest is history.

Have you ever fouled out of the game?

I have fouled out a couple of times, but it was never my fault. The first time, we had a ref who was still learning. She had never seen a star like me. I think she got mixed up because I was so fast. Another time, I fouled out because the other team was full of cheaters. I think they thought they would win if they got me off the court.

What do you do when you are on the bench?

I'm hardly ever on the bench. The only time I have been on the bench was when I fouled out.

There was one other time when I twisted my ankle.

I sometimes sit on the bench during halftime. It's a good place to eat an orange.

Do you have any tips?

Yes. Keep practicing. Shoot hoops whenever you get the chance. Make sure you can dribble with either hand. Also, don't worry if you're not tall. I'm not tall, yet, but I'm already a slam dunk magician.

Basketball Quiz
How Much Do You Know about Basketball?

Q1 How many players are on the court during a game of basketball?
A. 10. *B.* 12. *C.* 5.

Q2 What happens if you get fouled?
A. You start to smell. *B.* You get a free throw. *C.* You have chicken for lunch.

Q3 What is a time-out?
A. Time for lunch. *B.* Time spent in your room. *C.* When the coach stops play to talk to the team.

 **Q4** What is passing?

A. Racing past a much slower player. *B.* Throwing the ball to a teammate. *C.* Saying "no thanks" to your aunt's rutabaga casserole.

 **Q5** If you have made a layup, what have you done?

A. Gotten fired by the rest of the team. *B.* Thrown the ball away. *C.* Put the ball through the hoop off the backboard.

 **Q6** What is dribbling?

A. Drooling. *B.* Tracking mud and water all over the clean kitchen floor. *C.* Bouncing the ball down the court.

Q7 What is a turnover?
A. A type of pastry with apples or berries. **B.** Passing the ball to the opposition. **C.** Giving your basketball to a friend.

Q8 What is a steal?
A. Taking the ball from the opposition. **B.** Taking something that doesn't belong to you.
C. Hard metal.

Q9 How many referees are there in a game of basketball?
A. 5. **B.** 1. **C.** 2.

Q10 Which is the best basketball team in the world?
A. Team Toocool. **B.** Team Tony.
C. Team Dog.

ANSWERS

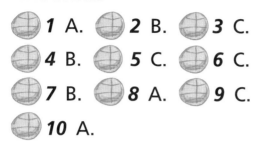

1 A. 2 B. 3 C.

4 B. 5 C. 6 C.

7 B. 8 A. 9 C.

10 A.

If you got ten questions right, call Toocool and the NBA. If you got more than five right, give Tony a call. If you got fewer than five right, buy a cushion for the bench.

TOOCOOL

Fishing Fanatic

At sunrise, **Toocool** will grapple with the giant of the deep—the marlin he dreams of catching. Has **Toocool** met his match? Let the battle begin.

Titles in the Toocool series